AMICUS ILLUSTRATED • AMICUS INK

DO YOU REALLY WANT TO MEET
A WOLF?

WRITTEN BY BRIDGET HEOS   ILLUSTRATED BY DANIELE FABBRI

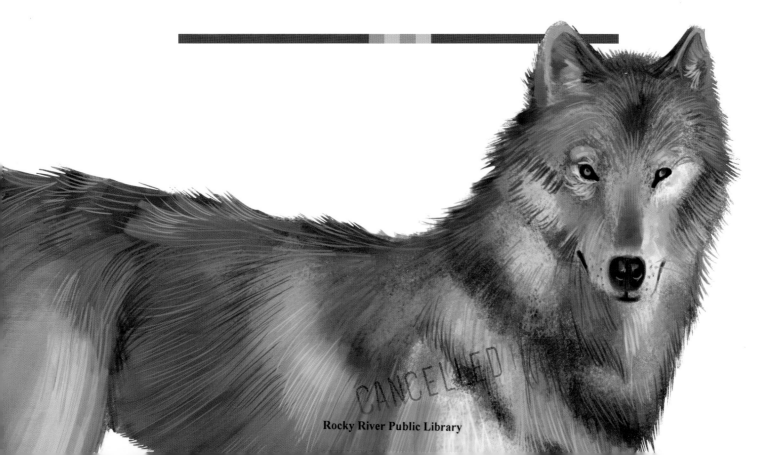

Amicus Illustrated and Amicus Ink
are imprints of Amicus
P.O. Box 1329
Mankato, MN 56002

Library of Congress Cataloging-in-Publication Data
Names: Heos, Bridget, author. | Fabbri, Daniele, 1978-
illustrator.
Title: Do you really want to meet a wolf? / by Bridget
Heos ; illustrated by Daniele Fabbri.
Description: Mankato, MN : Amicus Illustrated, [2016]
| Series: Do you really want to meet...wild animals? |
Audience: K to grade 3. | Description based on print
version record and CIP data provided by publisher;
resource not viewed.
Identifiers: LCCN 2015034751 (print) |
LCCN 2015037110 (ebook) |
ISBN 9781607539490 (library binding) |
ISBN 9781681521206 (pbk.) |
ISBN 9781681510675 (ebook)
Subjects: LCSH: Wolves—Behavior—Juvenile literature. |
Wolves—Juvenile literature.
Classification: LCC QL737.C22 (print) | LCC QL737.C22
H464 2016 (ebook) | DDC 599.773—dc23
LC record available at http://lccn.loc.gov/2015034751

Editor: Rebecca Glaser
Designer: Kathleen Petelinsek

Printed in the United States of America at Corporate
Graphics in North Mankato, Minnesota.

HC 10 9 8 7 6 5 4 3 2 1
PB 10 9 8 7 6 5 4 3 2 1

ABOUT THE AUTHOR

Bridget Heos lives in Kansas City with her husband, four children, and an extremely dangerous cat . . . to mice, anyway. She has written more than 80 books for children, including many about animals. Find out more about her at www.authorbridgetheos.com.

ABOUT THE ILLUSTRATOR

Daniele Fabbri was born in Ravenna, Italy, in 1978. He graduated from Istituto Europeo di Design in Milan, Italy, and started his career as a cartoon animator, storyboarder, and background designer for animated series. He has worked as a freelance illustrator since 2003, collaborating with international publishers and advertising agencies.

Wolves are beautiful. But you've heard of the "big, bad wolf," right? Do you really want to meet a wolf?

Wild wolves are actually afraid of people. And they rarely attack. Wolves are related to dogs, but they are not tame! Gray wolves used to live all over North America, Europe, and Asia. Now they live in only a few areas on those continents. Many live in Yellowstone National Park in Wyoming. Let's go!

Wolves are shy. We won't be able to see them up close. You brought your binoculars, right? There they are!

Wolves are social animals. An average pack has six to ten wolves, but a pack can be bigger or smaller. Looks like they're on the move now!

The wolves are chasing that elk! Wolves can smell their prey from miles away. They hunt large animals together as a pack. When they get close, they surround the elk and move in for the kill. Now it's dinnertime!

The alpha male and alpha female eat first. They are the parents and the pack leaders. Most other pack members are the alphas' pups, ones born this year and older siblings.

Finally, the other wolves get to eat. Boy, are they hungry! Wolves can eat 20 pounds (9 kg) of meat in a single meal! But what do the pups eat?

Don't worry. The pack takes care of its pups. Wolves are carnivores. But young pups aren't ready to chew meat. They get milk from their mother at first. Then the adults make them "baby food" by chewing up meat and spitting it out. Yum!

After the big meal, the adults are tired. But not
the pups! They're ready to wrestle and play!

It may look like fighting. But they are having fun! Even when they bite each other, it doesn't hurt. Their thick fur protects them. And the rough play prepares them to hunt one day.

It's gotten dark. The wolves are howling to each other. Listen. The pups are howling too. They learn from the adults.

You've seen many wolves today. But you still haven't met a wolf. Would you like to?

For that, we'll visit a wolf sanctuary. Wolves that need help are brought here to live. These wolves are more used to people, so you can see them up close.

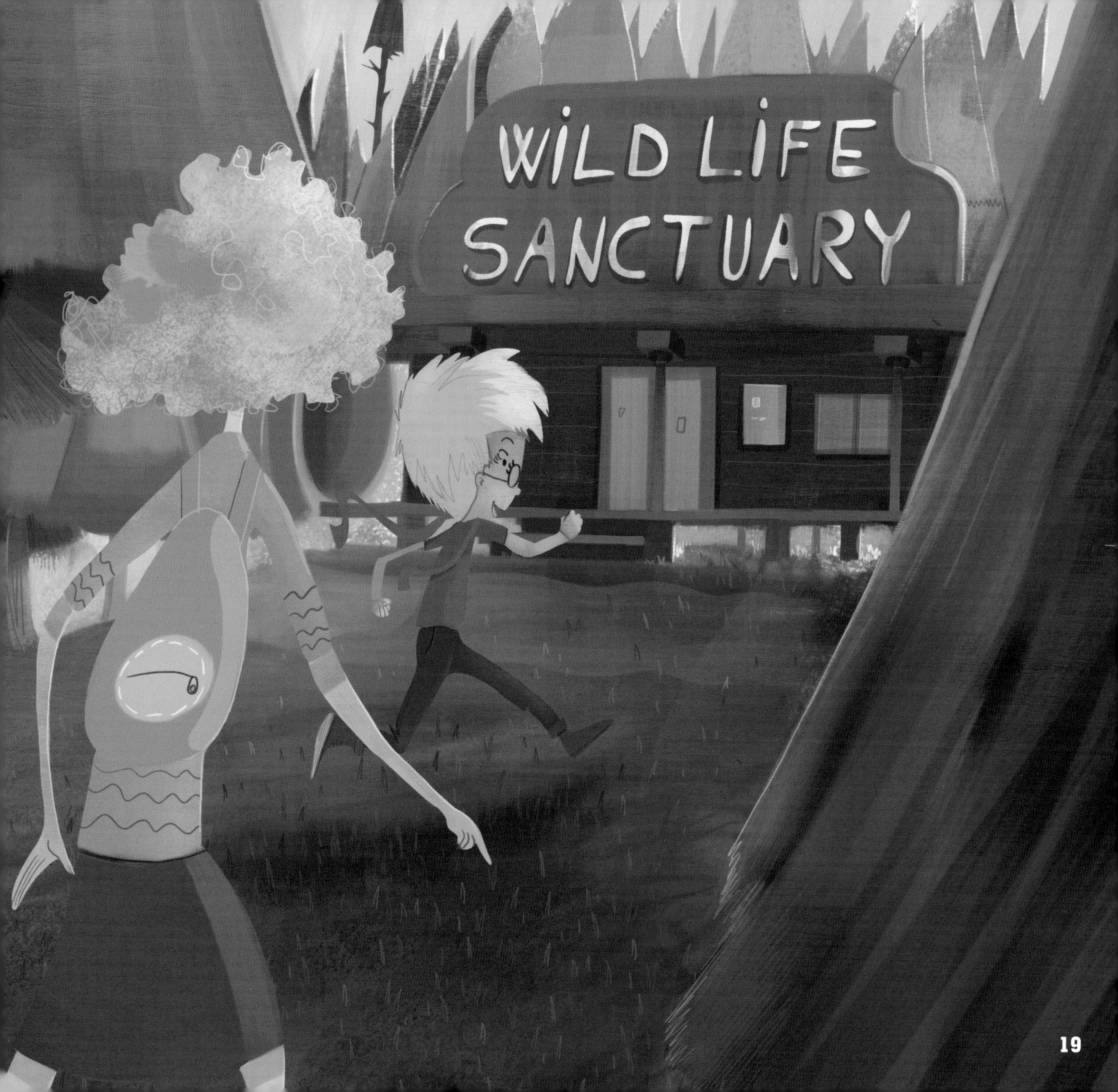
WILD LIFE
SANCTUARY

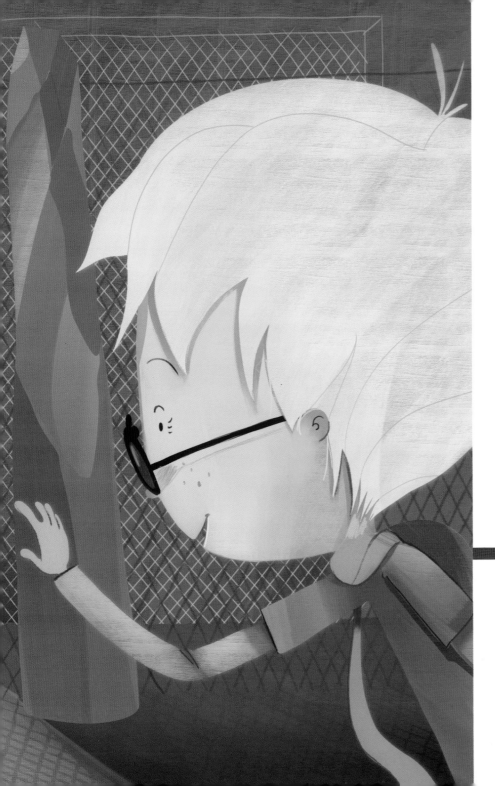

This wolf has been around people a lot. So he is not shy. Hello, big good wolf!

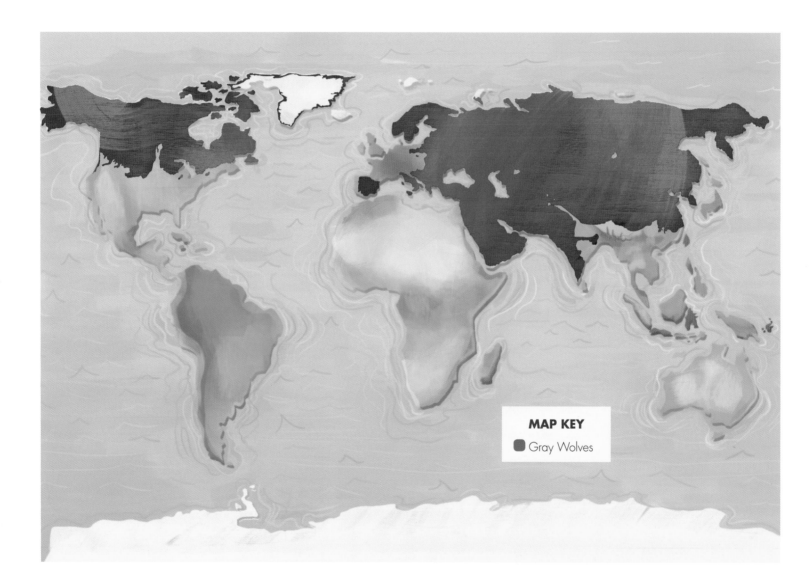

MAP KEY
● Gray Wolves

GLOSSARY

alpha A dominant individual in a pack of wolves; the alpha pair are usually the parents in the wolf pack.

carnivore An animal that eats meat.

pack A group of wolves that lives together.

prey An animal that is hunted by other animals for food.

pup A baby wolf.

social Living closely with other animals and interacting with them.

READ MORE

Furstinger, Nancy. *12 Mammals Back From The Brink*. North Mankato, Minn.: 12-Story Library, 2015.

Leaf, Christina. *Gray Wolves*. Minneapolis: Bellwether Media, 2015.

Marsh, Laura. **Wolves**. Washington, D.C.: National Geographic, 2012.

Shea, Adele. *Wolves in Danger*. New York: Gareth Stevens Publishing, 2014.

WEBSITES

BioKids Critter Catalog: Gray Wolf
http://www.biokids.umich.edu/critters/Canis_lupus/
Read more about gray wolves.

Kids' Planet: World Wide Wolves
http://www.kidsplanet.org/www/
Learn more about wolf populations worldwide with an interactive map.

National Geographic Kids: Gray Wolf
http://kids.nationalgeographic.com/animals/gray-wolf/
Learn more about gray wolves and see pictures of them in the wild.

PBS Kids DragonflyTV: Wolves
http://pbskids.org/dragonflytv/show/wolves.html
Watch Zach and Gerit's visit to the wolves at the wildlife center.

Every effort has been made to ensure that these websites are appropriate for children. However, because of the nature of the Internet, it is impossible to guarantee that these sites will remain active indefinitely or that their contents will not be altered.